Real Estate

The Beginner's Guide to Mastering Real Estate

Eric Alton

© **Copyright 2016 by Eric Alton - All rights reserved.**

This document is geared towards providing exact and reliable information in regards to the topic and issue covered. The publication is sold with the idea that the publisher is not required to render accounting, officially permitted, or otherwise, qualified services. If advice is necessary, legal or professional, a practiced individual in the profession should be ordered.

- From a Declaration of Principles which was accepted and approved equally by a Committee of the American Bar Association and a Committee of Publishers and Associations.

In no way is it legal to reproduce, duplicate, or transmit any part of this document in either electronic means or in printed format. Recording of this publication is strictly prohibited and any storage of this document is not allowed unless with written permission from the publisher. All rights reserved.

The information provided herein is stated to be truthful and consistent, in that any liability, in terms of inattention or otherwise, by any usage or abuse of any policies, processes, or directions contained within is the solitary and utter responsibility of the recipient reader. Under no circumstances will any legal responsibility or blame be held against the publisher for any reparation, damages, or monetary loss due to the information herein, either directly or indirectly.

The information herein is offered for informational purposes solely, and is universal as so. The presentation of the information is without contract or any type of guarantee assurance.

The trademarks that are used are without any consent, and the publication of the trademark is without permission or backing by the trademark owner. All trademarks and brands within this book are for clarifying purposes only and are the owned by the owners themselves, not affiliated with this document.

FOR ALL THOSE WHO SEEK FULFILLING AND
REWARDING ADVENTURES

TABLE OF CONTENTS

Introduction

Chapter 1: Getting Started

Chapter 2: What Can I Do With Real Estate?

Chapter 3: Starting Small

Chapter 4: Creating Connections and Partnerships

Chapter 5: Advantageous Opportunities

Chapter 6: The Art of Flipping

Conclusion

Introduction

Real estate can certainly be a trying, challenging, and fickle endeavor to both understand and master, though it's absolutely worth it in the long-run. Essentially, learning the basics of real estate and becoming an educated, pro-active member in the world of real estate comes down to one primary component: approach.

And when I say approach, I mean how you go about learning the basics of real estate before diving in, how you proceed with real estate-related transactions, and how you decide to pursue further real estate pursuits. In other words, the person who spends time learning about the market's movements and patterns, learning where and how to ask for assistance, learning about their numerous options, and learning how to generate the biggest profit through cost-effective means, will be the person who finds tremendous success.

Although this book is by no means an extensive and complex look into the world of real estate, it's a vital guide for beginners and those interested in pursuing a career in real estate, those interested in buying and selling property independently, or those simply interested in learning more about the fundamental sphere of real estate.

What makes this book unique from other books is its

approach to real estate—I've taken special care to address beginners of all forms, whether you're a beginner who is looking further into a career in real estate, or you're someone who has an interest in working independently and avoiding the commission fees that come from pulling in the assistance of an agent or Realtor. In other words, whatever your personal interests may be, I've tried to cater to each and every one of them throughout this book.

From Chapter 1 to the end of this book, you'll learn the basics of real estate. In Chapter 1, we'll start with an introduction to what exactly real estate is, outlining the different forms of property, the pros and cons of real estate involvement, and the crucial terms that you need to understand before moving forward. In Chapter 2, you'll discover two equally fine options in terms of getting involved with real estate-related endeavors—pursuing a career or hobby in real estate, or buying, selling, and generating profit from real estate pursuits independently. From there, you'll find an interesting introduction to something called AirBNB, an online outlet that lets property owners rent out property to tourists or traveling professionals. You'll quickly discover that I consider this option to be an excellent gateway to the real estate world, primarily because it gives you a feel for how property management works and how well you interact with clients (or renters). Chapter 4 is specifically dedicated to those interested in working independently. I offer some pros and cons of independent work, and suggest a helpful way to transition into independent real estate work. Chapter 5 revolves around better understanding residential real estate, commercial property, and raw land, and details how you can benefit from each property type and generate a substantial profit from each. Chapter 6 then concludes our discussion with an up-and-coming topic in the real estate world—property flipping. In this chapter I'll introduce 4 crucial elements of property flipping, and will suggest some helpful techniques and suggestions that go along with each.

Chapter 1—Getting Started

Appraisals. Contingencies. Adjustable rate mortgages. Buying vs. listing agents. Commissions. Abatement. Absorption rate. Amortization. These are just a few of the thousands of words that you'll hear tossed around during your involvement with real estate. Whether you're enrolled in pre-licensure Realtor courses, researching and interviewing with potential brokerages, buying properties with the help of a Realtor, selling real estate independently, or budgeting for a property flip, these are words you'll need to both know and understand in full. But before you do just that, a few additional things are in order. First and foremost, you need to have a basic understanding for what exactly we mean when we say real estate.

What Exactly is Real Estate?

For many of us, the term *real estate* conjures up the image of a quaint suburban house with a wrap-around porch, blue decorative shutters outlining the windows and, of course, a white picket fence that surrounds the property. This stereotypical image of a suburban house for sale is an image ingrained in many of our minds when we think about real estate, and that's perfectly okay—it absolutely is an example of real estate. But when we say real estate, we can mean a plethora of other things as well.

Real estate can be residential, like that quaint suburban house I just described, but it can also be commercial. And when I say commercial real estate, I mean any non-residential property used for profit-making purpose. Things like a mall or office building are examples of commercial real estate—they are non-residential buildings that people have bought and used with the intention of earning money.

Real estate doesn't always need to involve buildings, however. Real estate can also be properties that haven't yet been developed. In other words, real estate can be raw land. This raw land can then be used for a multitude of different purposes—if we purchase 500 acres of raw land and construct a neighborhood on it, then we've now created residential real estate. If we purchase 100 acres of raw land and build a 3-story shopping outlet on it, then we've created commercial real estate.

But if we break the term real estate down to its most basic form, all real estate implies is property, either in the form of buildings or land.

Who Are the Key Real Estate Players?

Let's quickly go back to my previous example, the one about the stereotypical suburban home for sale. When you think about the real estate "transaction" process,—the buying and selling of a house—who is involved? Well, there are, of course, the owners of the home and the buyers of the home. Who else? Maybe a Realtor? Perhaps several Realtors? Can you think of any more important figures involved during the buying and selling of a home? If you can, you're right—there are actually quite a few other crucial figures involves during the buying and selling process of real estate. So, real estate transactions aren't just between two people. Many people, actually, are involved in the process.

While the numbers and roles of active participants during real estate transactions may wary depending on the property type, size, and region, for example, you might expect to see involved figures such as:

- **Using owners:** Individuals or families who both live in and own residential real estate. These are the owners of single-family homes, for example.

- **Owners:** If you're an owner, but not a using owner (using owners live in the home), then you're someone who has probably made an investment in real estate. You own a property, but have rented or leased that property out to someone other than yourself.

- **Renters:** Renters are a bit different than owners, primarily because they don't own the property. They live in it, yes, but they simply rent out the rights to the property from the owner of the property.

- **Buyers/sellers:** When residential, commercial, or raw land real estate undergo a transaction, there is both a seller(s) and buyers(s) involved in the process, except perhaps when it comes to foreclosures (but we won't get into that right now).

- **Developers:** These are individuals, businesses, or corporations with hired professionals who prepare raw, undeveloped land for development.

- **Renovators:** Old properties, or properties in need of maintenance and renovation, are worked on by renovators. Renovators fix, remodel, and/or refurbish buildings before they appear on the market, either to ensure the property meets particular structural regulations, or to improve the value of the property and therefore sell the property at a higher market price.

- **Facilitators:** Many professionals fall under this category: Realtors, real estate brokers, banks, and lawyers. These are licensed or trained professionals who assist with the transaction of real estate, manage financial or legal affairs, or ensure the steps of buying and selling real estate are properly approached and followed through with.

The Pros and Cons of Getting Involved

The truth is, the pros and cons of getting involved with real estate will depend on what direction you're interested in taking. If you want to pursue a career in real estate, for example, perhaps as a Realtor, your pros and cons will differ from someone who, say, aspires to buy and sell real estate independently.

For those who are interested in the former option, you'll have the opportunity to be your own boss, create a flexible work schedule, and be selective about which clients you work with, but you'll first need to complete required training and pre-license courses, seek out employment in a growing professional field, and learn the ropes of the market and real estate business somewhat independently.

For those interested in buying and selling real estate independently, on the other hand, you'll eliminate the cost of Realtor commissions, secure the freedom in making your own real estate decisions, and generate a profit if all goes well, but you'll need to dedicate a large amount of your time and energy to buying/selling transactions, and will need to learn how the market works and reacts to certain events on your own.

But whatever position you find yourself in, or whatever direction you find yourself leaning toward in terms of real estate, it's important to know before you get started that the condition of the real estate market is fragile. Many of us witnessed this first hand during the 2008 financial crisis—the market crashed, the value of homes decreased, and the number of prospective real estate buyers experienced a drastic decline in so little time. Yes, entering the field of real estate can be a tricky thing, but it can also be a highly rewarding and profitable career endeavor or independent business venture. Knowing the risks of real estate, how the market functions, and how you can safely, effectively, and knowledgeable approach your real estate endeavors with specific skills and techniques, however, can certainly make the pros of real estate outweigh the cons.

Appreciation and Commission

Learning and understanding the slang, lingo, and more

formal terminologies of the real estate world will come with time (though you certainly can—and should—speed this process up by reaching out to others and building your vocabulary base on your own). If there are two terms and concepts that I think you should know before moving on, however, they're the concept of appreciation and the function of a commission.

You may already have a solid idea of how appreciation and commissions work in the real estate world—if you do, that's great. Feel free to skip ahead to the next chapter's discussion regarding your options with real estate. If you'd like to learn more about appreciation and/or commission, or would simply like a minute of review, spend a few minutes with the following section. You never know, you might find that your original understanding for these terms was a bit off.

So, that being said, what is appreciation and commission in the real estate world?

- **Appreciation:** Simply put, appreciation is the increase in value of property. For those just starting out in the real estate field, you should know that the appreciation of property is one of the best ways to secure profit.

    But let's rewind. Some readers might find themselves asking: how can property possibly increase in value?

Wouldn't living in a home cause the value of it to decrease? The short answer is no. Property, essentially, works in the opposite way of, say, a car. That is, as soon as you purchase a car and drive it off the dealership's lot, it depreciates—it instantly loses some of its original value. Houses, fortunately for us, work in the opposite way. Their value appreciates over time—it increases in value, at least generally speaking. The appreciation of property will be affected during times of financial crisis or economic uncertainty, as will most things in the real estate arena.

- **Commission:** This is the fee that a Realtor charges his or her clients for their assistance in selling their client's home. These fees are generally between 5% and 7% of the total selling price of the property. In a word, a commission isn't one set price—it depends on how much you sold your house for. Of this commission percentage, the listing agent (selling Realtor) and buying agent (the buying party's Realtor) generally split it. So, if the commission for a $250,000 property is 6%, the selling agent will receive 3% of $250,000, and the listing agent will also receive 3% of the $250,000 sell price.

    Commission percentages will, of course, vary depending on current market conditions, the selling price of the property, the scope of the work the Realtor has put into the buying/selling process, and the location of the property, to name a few. In other words, Realtors of multimillion dollar properties located in high-end neighborhoods will make a much larger commission than Realtors of 2 bedroom homes in need of maintenance.

Chapter 2—What Can I Do With Real Estate?

Surprisingly for some beginners, there are actually several different routes you can take upon entering the world of real estate. I won't focus on all of them in this book, though I do think two are worth our consideration. In other words, I'd like to introduce two equally fine real estate options that beginners should further look into and perhaps even pursue—either becoming a Realtor or buying and selling real estate independently.

I'd like to note here before moving on, however, that many of the following chapters in this book will be particularly helpful to those who decide to buy and sell real estate on their own (without the help or guidance of a Realtor). This is because you'll need to learn the entire process on your own. However, this isn't to say that the following chapters won't be helpful to those wanting to learn more about real estate or those who want to prepare themselves for a career or hobby in real estate. Whatever your path is, the following chapters will be of equal use.

Nonetheless, knowing what exactly your two best real estate options are is extremely helpful in this stage of the game, which is why I've included this chapter that details and outlines the basic process of becoming an agent/Realtor, or buying and selling real estate on your own.

Becoming an Agent

Becoming a licensed Realtor, which is different than a real estate agent believe it or not, won't require 8+ years of schooling like other professions, but you should expect to spend at least a year (but sometimes between 2-3 years) of prep work. What hoops you'll need to jump through, so to speak, before you become an agent will depend on the state in which you're pursuing a license, but most prospective agents and Realtors can expect to encounter the following process:

1. Pass background checks: This is the preliminary part of becoming an agent or Realtor, but it won't require too much effort or time on your part. A criminal background check will be performed, and biometric information such as your fingerprints may be recorded and placed on file.

2. Complete coursework and pass exam(s): This step is where the majority of your pre-agent, pre-licensure work begins and ends. With this step, you'll need to enroll in pre-licensure courses or education hours. The amount of courses required to receive your pre-license status will varying depending on which state you live in and wish to work in, but most people can expect to enroll and complete 3 courses. If your state based pre-licensure requires education hours rather than coursework, you can expect to dedicate about 150-200 hours of your time to education hours. At the end of your coursework or education hours, you'll need to pass an exam(s). Taking these exams require a bit of an investment—each exam will cost you about $80, so be prepared to pay some upfront money.

3. Seek and find a broker or brokerage: After you've completed your pre-licensure coursework/education hours, you'll need to research, interview with, and decide on a real estate broker or brokerage that you'd like to work with. Real estate brokerages are where licensed real estate agents and brokers work, and your partnership with a broker is required. Brokers undergo several more years of education and training than real estate agents, and therefore will assist you with any questions or concerns you have while you learn the ropes of real estate and conduct real estate transactions. To ensure you don't waste any time, be sure to contact brokerages before the end of your training/education period.

As you research and interview with potential brokers and brokerages, you might find the following guidelines and questions to be of use during the process. Consider yourself and/or ask brokers the following:

- What size brokerage do I want to work for? What do I feel comfortable with?

- What is this brokerage interested in, and what are their values? Do these values and interests align with mine?

- What is the brokerage's reputation in the community? If applicable, what is its national reputation?

- What does this particular broker or brokerage offer to employees in my position? How can they assist me in my career? How will they better me as a real estate agent?

Remember, this stage in the process should be an interview stage—for both you *and* the brokers you meet with. Shop around for potential brokers and brokerages until you feel comfortable and find a brokerage that mirrors your real estate interests and personal/professional values.

4. Get licensed and buy insurance: Once you've settled upon a brokerage to work with, it's time to get your license. You'll need to pass state and/or national exams in order to secure your license, and doing so will cost you some money—you can expect to pay roughly $200 in expenses: exam fees, paying board dues, MLS dues, operating expenses, etc. These are oftentimes called continuing costs.

While you're at it, you'll also want to consider getting Error and Omission Insurance (E&O insurance). This is a professional liability insurance that protects you against claims and complaints made by clients regarding inadequate work or negligent actions.

5. Become a Realtor (optional): I noted earlier that being a real estate agent is different from being a Realtor. You'll need a license to be an agent, but you'll need to complete additional steps in order to gain the "Realtor" title. Fortunately, doing so isn't too complicated—to become a Realtor, you'll need to:

- Join the National Association of Realtors (NAR)
- Choose an affiliated brokerage to work with
- Attend meetings and meet requirements formed and proposed by your local chapter

6. Meet "Education Continuation" standards: Again, education continuation standards will vary depending on the state in which you live and have earned your Realtor license, but you should expect to be required to attend "education continuation" courses every couple of years after you've earned your license. This will allow you to re-new your license and ensure your real estate knowledge is up-to-date.

Further Suggestions

- **Create a budget and fund:** Pursing a career in real estate will require some upfront investments, though relatively minor in the grand scheme of things. I mentioned several of these small investments earlier, but to reiterate, you'll need to pay for pre-licensure courses/education hours, association fees, exam fees, board dues, and perhaps even business cards and advertising expenses. Creating a fund before you enter the field is important because you're working in a field in which your income thrives from commission. If you're not actively selling houses and earning a commission, you're not actively earning an income.

   When you're just getting started, you can't always expect to jump right into buying and selling transactions, and therefore make an immediate profit. This is why having a fund established is crucial. I'd recommend having 6 month's money already in your savings account before getting started so that you can continue to pay monthly expenses and live comfortably while you transition into the field and grow your client base.

- **Find and work with a mentor:** Having a mentor in the field will make your transition process go a lot smoother, but they'll also, perhaps more importantly, help you dive into the ever-important networking environment synonymous with real estate. They'll help you create partnerships with other Realtors and expand your cliental base.

  You'll need to work alongside your mentor in many instances, which means splitting commission, but he or she will steer you in the right direction in terms of finding buying/selling contracts, and will give you the crucial boost in creating and fostering personal networks, partnerships, and connections. In short, keep your mentor handy until you feel comfortable conducting transactions and interacting with clients on your own.

Working Independently

Although both real estate agents and independent buyers and sellers of real estate are grouped under the same umbrella, so to speak, their paths differ more than you'd think. A real estate agent, as we saw in the previous section, for example, has a set, step-by-step process that they need to complete before securing their Realtor license. It's a relatively simple, though sometimes time-consuming, 6 step process. Becoming an independent buyer and seller of real estate, on the other hand, doesn't follow such a neat, organized, and regimented step-by-step process.

Because of its independent nature, private buyer and sellers have the opportunity to make the rules as they go, at least in some ways. You can avoid dishing out commission fees to real estate agents, eliminate the need to pay the many fees real estate agents pay on a yearly basis, and avoid the required coursework/education hours/continuing education standards and associated fees. Keep in mind, though, that you can't go into real estate blind—avoiding coursework and education hours doesn't mean you can avoid educating yourself on the real estate market, how successful transactions are approached and completed, and how to find success in the world of real estate. And let me be the first to warn you: you won't be able to do this in a few hours. For some it takes weeks, even months, to merely scrape the surface. Keep that in mind as you move forward with your reading.

If you're considering buying/selling real estate independently, however, you'll want to review the following information. These are the crucial elements of privately selling a property that many first-time sellers tend to overlook or fail to fully consider:

- **Renovating, price, description, and photos:** Let's start with the renovating element of selling a property because it's fairly simple: do it. No, you don't need to drop thousands if your property is already in a good condition, but you should put a bit of effort into getting a new coat of paint on the walls, steam-cleaning carpets, or updating appliance. You'll want the property to feel as new as possible, but don't need to break your bank account to do so.

Setting the price of your property can get a bit tricky, as this is where the help of a Realtor comes into play. Independent sellers are fully capable of setting a competitive asking price, however, so don't be too put off by this step. Do your research. Look for comparable properties and see what price they are on the market for. Browse online and look for sold price histories for properties similar to yours and in a nearby area. Just be wary of overpricing (and the temptation to overprice as well).

You'll need to spend some time when writing the description for your property and taking photos of the property. Again, this is something that a Realtor handles for his or her clients. Rest assured, though. Descriptions and photos are relatively easy. Get your hands on a real estate booklet (you can often find these for free at the entrance of stores, malls, and sometimes restaurants) or simply look online. Take note of how Realtors write property descriptions, what words they use, and what features of the properties they focus on. The same idea goes for photos—take note of the angles of property photos, how many there are, and if any rooms in particular are the most photographed. Essentially, you want to mimic what a trained, licensed Realtor is doing.

- **How and where to market your home:** Unfortunately, many online agents don't accept listings from private property sellers. And if they do, it's usually at a cost. However, there are websites that allow "for sale by owner" postings. You might find it helpful to check out **Fizber.com.** This is a website that allows home owners to post property descriptions, photos, and details—for free. I personally recommend Fizber.com because when you create a property post on this site, your listing will automatically appear on additional online real estate websites including, but not limited to: Zillow, Trulia, Yahoo real estate, HomeFinder, and craigslist.

- **Making time for organizing and conducting viewings:** Because you're working on your own, you'll need to handle all viewing-related tasks. You'll need to call back interested viewers, arrange viewing times, and conduct the actual viewing yourself. There are two things to keep in mind as you prepare for this stage of the selling process: 1.) you need to make yourself available for viewers and have a flexible schedule, and 2.) you need to know the details about your property and how to sell it. Facts and details that you'll absolutely want to familiarize yourself with beforehand include things like:

- Lot acreage

- Year built

- Nearby amenities, community areas, schools, public transportation

- Electric/heating features (gas, natural gas, oil, etc.)

- Exterior features (sprinkler system, gutters, shingles, etc.)

- Utilities connections (washer hookup, cable in rooms, etc.)

Because independent buyers and sellers of real estate don't have a simple step-by-step process that real estate agents do, many of the following chapters will be specifically geared toward introducing what directions independent buyers and sellers can pursue in the world of real estate. Of course, the following information will be helpful to those seeking a career in real estate, or simply interested in learning more about it, too.

Chapter 3—Starting Small

Real estate can be a highly rewarding and personally fulfilling career, business, or personal venture. But getting to the rewarding, fulfilling stages of real estate involvement can take some time—whether you've decided to earn your Realtor license or want to sell properties on your own, the entire process will be a learning process.

When you're surrounded by fellow real estate agents, Realtors, or brokers at holiday parties, social gatherings, or orientation meetings, you might hear a lot of talk about how each person found themselves in the field of real estate. For some, it was an achievable career objective that didn't require years of higher education. For others, licensure, education hours, and continuing education costs were relatively small fees that they found worth the investment in the grand scheme of things. Still, for others, real estate was something they simply enjoyed—they loved talking about the characteristics of each property to prospective buyers, and they appreciated the challenge of verbally selling a property. What you probably won't hear during these conversations, however, is this: don't immediately dive into real estate; start small.

"There's an excellent option that lets you test the waters of real estate, so to speak, while also giving you first-hand experience working with "clients" and helping you secure a passive income in the process."

I know what you're probably thinking: why would I start small when I already have the knowledge, tools, and skills required to find and achieve success? Or maybe: what can be smaller than starting off without a license, any coursework or education hours under my belt, or any affiliation with a real estate brokerage?

Becoming an agent or selling properties on your own probably won't take you years to achieve, fortunately, but it certainly still requires some sort of time commitment on your behalf. Before you delve into the real estate world, you should make sure that this career or venture is suitable for *you*. Fortunately, there's an excellent option that lets you test the waters of real estate, so to speak, while also giving you first-hand experience working with "clients" and helping you secure a passive income in the process.

And remember our discussion in Chapter 2 about creating a fund *before* you begin working as an agent or begin buying and selling properties independently? Well, this "start small" option will allow you to create and add to this fund, putting you in the perfect financial and personal position should you reaffirm your interest in becoming an agent or independent buyer/seller. So, what exactly is this "start small" option that I keep going on about?

AirBNB

AirBNB is actually quite the up-and-coming income-producing opportunity, so odds are many readers might have heard about it already. If you haven't, airBNB is an online marketplace that helps those seeking to rent out their property connect with those looking for either short-term or long-term accommodations (although short-term accommodations are generally what renters are seeking). AirBNB is a virtual place that lets hosts (people like you who own property that is ready to rent out) post pictures and details of the property, approve renters who book travel dates, and earn a little extra money from a property you otherwise wouldn't be using. It's helpful to think of your property listed on AirBNB's website as a substitute for a hotel—AirBNB is very popular among tourists and business professionals who are looking for more comfortable short-term travel accommodations with a more home-like feel.

The great news about this website is that it's available in over 190 countries, which means your property, if you'd like it to be, is made available to interested renters coming from, well, 190 different countries.

Why AirBNB is a Smart Move

AirBNB is a less risky, more easily approachable way of profiting from real estate for beginners or less experienced individuals who want to pursue real estate independently or want to avoid Realtor commission fees. Although you probably won't find the same level of success (and income) as you would working as an agent or selling and buying real estate, this option is an excellent introduction to the world of real estate, and does help you create a savings fund (which you'll probably need to pull from when you do finally begin working as an agent or begin selling/buying independently).

But now that I've introduced AirBNB, let me reiterate why this is a great option for those interested in real estate:

- **It doesn't require a huge investment** like purchasing law rand, commercial property, or residential property would (we'll talk about these options in the following chapters). Actually, if you've already got a property that you're not currently living in—a second home, a small condo, a property passed down as an inheritance, for example—you don't really need to make any major investments at all. You're simply making money off of what you already own. Sure, some slight renovations or modifications might be in order every once and a while (new paint, new carpet, perhaps), but these won't break the bank.

- **Any property will work:** This is especially important for non-property owning individuals: you don't need to own or invest in a house—small or large—in order to reap the benefits of airBNB. Investing in an apartment, condo, cabin, or even a 2-room trailer-home will work. And, it doesn't need to be anything fancy. Sometimes tourists just want a simple furnished property close to tourist attractions.

- **You're protected:** AirBNB's Host Guarantee program provides protection for up to $1,000,000 in damages to covered property, in case guests damage or cause destruction (in rare cases) to your property. You'll need to read the fine print for this section in order to understand what damages are covered under the program and what you'll need to do beforehand in order to ensure you're covered, but I'd recommend looking further into this option. However, hosts have the ability to choose which renters they rent to, which means if you're a good judge in character, you can essentially eliminate the risk of destruction and skip over the cost of the protection program.

- **You're securing a passive income:** The income that you secure from renting means you can add to your savings account, an account you'll probably end up needing to withdraw from and utilize while you undergo the real estate agent licensure process or work toward buying and selling property independently. Moreover, adding to your savings account means you'll have the funds readily available so that you can purchase and invest in larger properties that sell for higher market prices. It's a win-win, really.

Chapter 4—Creating Connections and Partnerships

Finding success in the world of real estate revolves primarily around communication, connections, and partnerships. Of course, the degree to which you pursue these elements will vary depending on what you intend to do with real estate—an independent seller will need strong communication and personal skills, but, because they're working on their own, they'll be able to get away without needing to form lasting connections and partnerships with Realtors and brokers (although this, too, is highly advised). If you're planning on becoming an agent or Realtor, on the other hand, foregoing connections and partnerships just won't cut it. You'll *need* to pursue lasting partnerships with successful Realtors. You'll *need* to form concrete connections with brokers. You'll *need* to find a mentor who will guide you through the process and introduce you to bigger, more effective networks of people—realtors, brokers, brokerages, and clients.

What I'm trying to say is this: this chapter is important—don't skip over it.

Although I won't be talking specifically about how you can improve your communication and interpersonal skills with others, I'll introduce and discuss a topic that is very important, especially for the individuals reading this who are interested in buying and selling real estate independently. (Creating connections and partnerships will come much more easily for those planning to become real estate agents or Realtors—especially if you find a mentor—so I won't spend too much time directing this conversation to that specific group of readers).

Transitioning into Independence

It might come as a bit of a surprise, but individuals hoping to buy and sell real estate independently might find they need some help when they're first getting started. It's actually something that happens quite frequently—successful independent buyers and sellers of real estate often work with a Realtor for a few times before embracing the challenge of handling real estate on their own. This is because real estate can be a tricky task, but the challenges that come with it are often overcome more effectively when individuals have worked with a professional beforehand, have seen how they approach real estate endeavors, and understand how to think like a Realtor.

So, if you haven't yet picked up on it, I'd recommend that those interested in buying and selling real estate independently work with a Realtor, at least in the beginning. Let's discuss this in more detail.

The Pros and Cons

It does seem rather odd, though, doesn't it—me recommending that those interested in buying and selling real estate independently work with a Realtor? I'll be the first to admit that what I'm saying does sound a bit contradictory, but, if you do decide to accept this advice, you'll quickly discover the benefits of doing so. Of course, there are disadvantages to this approach as well. Here are some quick, important things that you'll want to keep in mind as you begin to consider this strategy:

Pro #1

You'll get a smooth transition into independent work: If you're interested in buying and selling real estate for profit on your own, but aren't entirely confident about the process or simply aren't ready to do it entirely by yourself, that's no problem. In fact, I'd even consider it a red flag if you didn't feel this way when first beginning to think about navigating the world of real estate. Working with a Realtor or real estate agent, even just in part, will give you the opportunity to ask questions, voice concerns, and simply *learn* the structure and movement of the real estate market. The knowledge you gather from your partnership, even if it's only for one or two transactions, will be knowledge that you simply can't learn from navigating the internet or reading online articles.

Pro #2

You're supported and protected: Real estate is risky, and it becomes even riskier when you're buying and selling property without the proper training or advice from an educated agent or Realtor. Many first-time independent buyers and sellers find that they want to feel more supported during transactions, and even find that the opposing party of buyers or sellers sometimes dominate the transaction or manipulate their decisions. Working with a Realtor, however, means you're supported during the entire transaction process—they'll show you how to handle clients and how to stand firm during the price negotiation process, among other things. And sometimes, you simply need to feel supported just a few times before you feel confident doing it on your own.

Pro #3

It's a safe way to test the real estate waters, so to speak: Some independent buyers and sellers will quickly find that the world of real estate is not what they imagined it to be, for various reasons. Your first buy/sell transaction might possibly be your last. If you're not entirely sure how your real estate experience will go, and if you think this might be a possibility for you, working with a Realtor is highly advantageous—they'll help you conduct and finalize your transaction quickly and effectively so you can exit quicker, if need be. Working with a Realtor or agent for the first couple of times will also allow you to ask questions and get answers if you find yourself on the border of moving forward or turning back with your real estate endeavors.

Con #1

A Realtor's services will cost you: I mentioned this in an earlier chapter, but the income that a real estate agent or Realtor makes during buying/selling transactions depends almost entirely on commission—an amount of money that is paid to agents for their help, and is calculated by finding, generally speaking, 5-7% of the selling/buying price of a property. You'll need to pay up when it comes time to pay, but, if you look at the pros listed above, you might find that it's worth it in the end.

- **How to make it better**: Because the commission percentage an agent receives is based upon the buying/selling price of a property, you can somewhat control how much you owe. Buying smaller properties, for example, usually means the commission you pay your agent will be smaller as well, which means you won't get bogged down in commission fees.

The Logistics of Finding an Agent

Remember, it's your time and money we're talking about it; don't gamble it away.

Hopefully you're beginning to feel convinced about working with a Realtor or agent when you're first getting started with independent buying and selling transactions. No, it won't *technically* be independent at first, but it will keep you protected, help you feel supported, and allow you to test the real estate waters, ask questions, voice concerns, and learn the ropes of the real estate world—and all with reduced risks and (hopefully) less frustrations.

If this option sounds like something you're interested in—and I personally hope it is—I'd suggest finding and working with an agent or Realtor for the first 1-3 real estate transactions you pursue. I haven't given you a solid number because, well, this number will vary. Some people will learn the structure of the real estate market and the transaction process quicker than others, though either speed is equally fine. Real estate isn't something that should be rushed, so if you're still not feeling entirely confident working on your own after the 3rd time, for example, continue to work with your Realtor until you finally do. Remember, it's your time and money we're talking about it; don't gamble it away.

Nonetheless, as you work toward finding and temporarily working with a Realtor, you'll want to keep a few things in mind. First and foremost:

- **Always conduct your initial meeting like an interview:** You want to temporarily work with an agent or Realtor who has the same interests as you, who you get along with, and who you know will work for *you* (someone who has your personal interests in mind). Because of this, you'll need to learn about potential agents and ask important questions during your initial meeting. Get a feel for what each agent values, what they know, and how they propose to help you personally.

Once you've relayed your interests, goals, and budget,

- **Open the floor up for your questions and concerns:** If you've conducted your meeting with a potential agent like an interview, as I suggested above, then it's only natural that questions will follow.

Knowing what questions to ask a potential agent or Realtor, however, can be particularly difficult for the first-timer. Rest assured, though. The following is a list of helpful questions that you should always ask a prospective agent or Realtor during your initial meeting:

1. How long have you been licensed for, and how long have you been selling for?

2. What additional credentials do you have?

- Realtors, specifically, will typically have additional credentials that separate them from others. There are additional certifications that agents can secure such as:

    - **CRS:** (Certified Residential Specialist)— additional training in managing residential real estate, specifically.

    - **ABR:** (Accredited Buyer's Representative)— additional training in representing buyers in real estate transactions, specifically.

3. Do you have a list of recent clients or references that I can contact? Does your brokerage have an online website that includes reviews written by previous clients?

4. Do you have a list of properties you've listed and sold within the past year? If so, can I have a copy to review?

5. Have you sold similar properties to mine in the past, in terms of location, price, etc.? If so, how long were those properties, on average, on the market for before being sold?

6. Are there similar properties to mine for sale in the area, currently?

- This is a great question to ask because it'll quickly show you whether or not an agent is familiar with your specific area and if they are on top of market movements. **Always ask this question.** If an agent isn't able to list at least 2 properties (without needing to reference anything), then I'd recommend searching elsewhere.

As you conduct your interview-like meeting with a prospective agent and ask them the above questions, keep in mind that they're certain things to look out for as well. For example, you'll want to watch out for, and perhaps even avoid:

- **Agents who do real estate part-time or on the side:** Working with a part-time agent might be a good idea if you're trying to wean yourself off of working with an agent and trying to transition yourself into the process of buying and selling property independently, but working with a part-time agent isn't generally the best approach if you need an agent who will play an active role when you're just starting out.

- **Agents who suggest the highest selling price for your property:** It's certainly a tempting offer to work with an agent who promises to market your property for the highest price, but it's not always the best option. My advice is to consult at least 3 different agents (from 3 different brokerages) about the price they'd list your property for, and to not automatically lean toward the agent who suggests the highest price. Overpricing generally turns potential buyers away, and therefore means your property takes longer to sell. Remember: properties that sit on the market are a bit of an eyesore to both Realtors and buyers because it suggests something is *wrong*.

- **Agents who aren't familiar with your neighborhood:** Always find a neighborhood expert, regardless of whether you're selling residential property, commercial property, or raw land. If you're a buyer, an agent who's familiar with your area will know which properties offer the best value without the added cost. If you're selling, working with an agent who's familiar with an area means they might have contact with other local Realtors who have clients in search of properties similar to yours. Involving yourself with a local agency is key here because real estate thrives on networking and personal connections.

Chapter 5—Advantageous Opportunities

Although it certainly can be complicated and messy at times, real estate is a wonderful pursuit for ambitious individuals to pursue if they're in search of securing a profit. Property, regardless of its type, appreciates over time, thus providing excellent long-term investment opportunities or short-term flipping ventures. Take your pick—the options are endless, but keep in mind that some real estate options are simply more beneficial than other real estate options.

If you're interested in securing a profit or income from real estate-related endeavors—whether you're planning on becoming an agent or interested in working independently—your best bet is to dive into areas of real estate that are in current and high demand. These opportunities might vary depending on where you live and the current economy in which you're planning to buy or sell, but there are three crucial categories of real estate that most individuals can depend upon. These categories are residential, commercial, and raw land.

I've introduced these three categories earlier on in this book, but I'd like to now spend a bit more time with each one of them. With that being said, in this chapter I'll introduce a little about each category of real estate, why they're such profitable real estate pursuits, and how you can use each property type to your advantage.

Residential

When we think about real estate, most of us imagine homes for sale. This takes us all the way back to chapter 1 when we talked about the stereotypical image of the white picket-fenced, blue-shuttered home for sale. Well, this form of property is considered residential property, or residential real estate.

In other words, residential real estate is:

- Any property containing either a single-family or multi-family building.

- A structure made specifically for occupation, and not for business purposes.

Simple enough, right? Fortunately, dealing with residential property and generating a profit from independently buying/selling residential property is a moderately simple task, too (that is, with the right amount of knowledge, experience, patience, and time-commitment). Let me explain.

For independent buyers and sellers of residential real estate, making investment decisions for residential property can be a somewhat difficult process if you don't know exactly what to look for. That's what this section is here to help you do—learn what advantageous qualities and elements to look for while pursuing potential residential real estate investments.

Up-and-coming Areas

Set your attention on residential properties that are situated close to or surrounded by up-and-coming neighborhoods and communities.

First and foremost, you'll want to set your attention on residential properties that are situated close to or surrounded by up-and-coming neighborhoods and communities. At this point, it's important for me to say this: you don't always need to lean toward property that is located in already established and well-developed areas. Why? Well, as new homes are built around your residential property, your property automatically (and sometimes drastically) increases in value— it appreciates. As new homes are built, current, older homes tend to undergo renovations, shopping areas are constructed, additional schools/school systems are added to support growing student populations, public transportation increases, and new community centers pop up here and there. In other words, with community growth, the value and desirability of your property increases. Something to keep in mind, though: when these elements start to crumble—if schools lose funding, shopping areas suffer economically, businesses close down, public transport is reduced due to budget cuts—the value of your residential property will decrease as well.

Essentially, my advice is to focus your attention on residential properties that are located in or surrounded by blossoming communities that you feel confident will be stable over the course of at least 5 years (this will give you ample time to make minor renovations, allow your property to appreciate in value, and sell it before it depreciates as the result of a weakened or crumbling community). The location of your property and the neighborhood it's situated in is crucial.

Single and Multi-family Properties

Unlike commercial property and raw land, with residential real estate, you have two primary categories: single-family property and multi-family property. These two properties are exactly what they sound like—a single-family home is occupied by, well, one singular family, and a multi-family home, is, well, you probably guessed it by now. Honing in on one or both of these residential property categories (buying and renting them out) is an excellent profit-generating investment. One statistic offered by the U.S Census American Community Survey suggests that there are currently 14.9 million single-family homes that are occupied by renters. Essentially, that's 14.9 million opportunities for you to make a profit by purchasing and renting out a single-family home to renters.

Of course, there are both pros and cons to this option of being a landlord to a single-family or multi-family home. Here's what you need to know:

Pro #1:

Decision-making freedom: As a landlord figure of either single or multi-family properties, you'll gain the freedom to select tenants, set weekly or monthly rental prices without restrictions (though keep in mind that too high of a rental price won't attract renters) and avoid fees that go toward additional property managers.

Con #1:

More responsibility: As someone who is renting out residential property, you'll gain quite a few responsibilities—

you'll be in charge of handling urgent repairs and communicating with renters quickly and efficiently. You'll also have to deal with the rather large initial investment that came from purchasing the residential property you're now renting out. This latter responsibility is probably the biggest one, since you won't really start to generate a profit until 8-12 years into your investment. Don't let this deter you from looking further into this option though—and keep in mind that setting the rent at a higher price means you'll generate profit quicker, too.

Commercial

We live in residential properties, but we work in or deal with commercial property on a daily basis as well. For those a bit confused as to what commercial property entails, commercial property is:

- Any structure designed to create income, maintain business, or generate capital gain.

So, like we discussed earlier on, commercial property can be malls or other shopping plazas. It can be office buildings, dentist offices, hospitals, or movie theaters. If you go there for recreational fun, entertainment, business, or shopping, it's commercial real estate.

When it comes to commercial real estate, there are specific things you'll want to know before deciding to invest, buy, or sell. What I'm going to recommend for commercial real estate is a bit like my recommendation for residential property—look for property in up-and-coming neighborhoods. However, there are some slight changes to my recommendation. But, let me rewind—I'm getting a bit ahead of myself here.

Location and Intended Consumers

When you're thinking about purchasing (or even building) commercial real estate in hopes to generate some sort of profit, look for properties situated in good locations. By good locations, I mean areas where population is increasing, communities are expanding, and additional neighborhoods are being constructed. Of course, you'll need to consider what type of commercial property you're purchasing when it comes to this step. Here's a hypothetical example of what I mean:

Let's say you've always been interested in purchasing an arcade. You loved going to them as a child, and still love going to them with your own children. You've been keeping tabs on the arcade-economy (financially-speaking, arcades have experienced a 5-year upwards trend in profit), and you think now is the right time to buy. At this point, you know that you want to purchase an arcade, and that you have 3 different property locations in mind—in a city neighborhood, in a shopping plaza located in the center of a rural vacation town, or on the beach-side ocean-walk.

But which location is the best? To determine this, you'll need to consider who your intended demographic is. In other words, who are your consumers? Well, they're families with children, mostly, and generally young ones at that. Knowing this, you can eliminate the city neighborhood. You know have two options left—the shopping plaza in the vacation town or the beach-side location. But which one is the best choice? Always consider the amount of yearly visitors—you can even find statistics on this quite easily online or by visiting the local town hall or tourist center. In most cases, however, the beach-side location would draw in the most families with young children, which means the commercial arcade property situated on the beach-front ocean-walk is your best, most profitable option.

Potential for Quick Improvements

You'll of course what to consider the location of your commercial real estate, and how well-situated it is in terms of your intended consumer or demographic, but you'll also want to consider something else: purchase commercial properties that can easily undergo improvements. That's right—you don't need to purchase brand-new commercial properties in order to generate profit (because this will usually cost you a pretty penny). If you're on a budget, my recommendation is to purchase commercial property that is simply in good shape, property that, once you give it a nice new coat of paint, maybe replace a few floors, and tidy up around the exterior, looks much better than it did before you started. The reason why is this: improvements, even minor ones, greatly contribute to appreciation, and when a property appreciates, you generate a larger profit when you sell. So, don't shy away from commercial properties that need a fresh coat of paint. Don't fear properties that could benefit from having the dirt-driveway and walk-way replaced with a cement one. Don't be put off my properties that don't have a clean, outwardly appearance—adding shrubs, replacing patches of grass, and lining walk-ways with stone pavers and flowers are quick, simple, and cost-effective fixes that quickly and painlessly add value.

Raw Land

Investors often shy away from raw land because generating profit from it can sometimes seem like a looming task—purchase undeveloped land and turn it into something that is useful, profitable, and successful. Though developing raw land might require more involvement on your end then would, say, purchasing residential property, you've also got some more freedom. But before we move forward, let's start off by explaining that raw land is:

- Land or property in its natural state, meaning it has yet to be developed.

- Free of any man-made improvements, changes, or modifications.

I mentioned that raw land brings with it more options. This is because raw land can be developed into either residential property or commercial property. Depending on your interests and budget, it's entirely your pick. So, the main idea behind purchasing and investing in raw land is this: purchase undeveloped land and develop it.

Land Near Cities

Of course, developing raw land isn't as clear-cut as I've made it sound so far. Much like with residential and commercial real estate, there are certain elements that you'll want to consider when purchasing and developing raw land real estate. My recommendation is to seek out pieces of land located close to or centrally situated in cities or metropolis areas that are currently expanding. The faster the expansion of the nearby city, the better it is for you and your wallet. This is because the land surrounding expanding cities becomes more valuable because of its growing potential. Urban sprawl is a real thing, just look at any large city and see how groups of houses and businesses tend to spread out and expand beyond the city center. Take advantage of this by purchasing property located within this area.

Beat Other Developers

You might always want to gear your attention toward raw property that is valuable or attractive to other developers. This is great for two reasons. First, developers are always looking for more land to develop, and having highly desirable land that other developers want gives you the upper hand. You'll be surprised at just how much money developers will offer you for your raw land. Second, and if you follow this first step, you simply need to purchase the land, not develop it. This will save you quite a considerable amount of cash, but will also allow you to generate a substantial amount of cash for the sale of your raw land to developers.

Chapter 6—The Art of Flipping

Most of us have probably stumbled upon, at least at one time or another, a television program that revolves around the growing trend of property flipping, especially residential property flipping. If you're not quite familiar with what flipping is, how it works, or why it's a potentially advantageous, profit-generating real estate venture, but are interested in learning more about it, pay close attention to this chapter. You'll find a simple but helpful introduction to what I call the "art of flipping," and will learn everything you need to know about flipping in order to get started, or at least decide if property flipping is something you'd be interested in further pursuing.

With that short blimp of an introduction out of the way, a flipped property refers to property that was bought and sold within 12 months of purchase. During this 12 month time period, renovations are done to the property—some drastic, some minor—in order to increase the value of the property, sell it for more than the initial purchase price, and generate a substantial profit in the process.

From this brief, introductory explanation, you might have been able to pull a few things away from this already. First, you might have noticed the rather limited time-span of this endeavor—12 months. That's right—to successfully flip a property, you've got to purchase it (and perhaps get approved for a loan even before that happens), set a budget, create a strict timeline, hire contractors, finish all planned renovations, put it on the market, conduct open-houses, negotiate a selling price, and finally sell it. In other words, you've got *a lot* to do during that short, 12-month period. From this, you're hopefully starting to gather that flipping is a rather hands-on and time-consuming venture. You'll probably have a hard time managing a flip while working full-time, in other words, though it's certainly not impossible.

If you're in a financial position that responsibly allows you to pursue a property flip, or if you're simply a time-management prodigy, then pursuing a property flip or flips might be a good real estate route for you to learn more about and even pursue. If this sounds like something you're interested in, do continue on with this chapter. In the following section, you'll find several crucial steps and suggestions about successfully managing and completing a 12-month property flip, all without taking unreasonable risks, struggling with budgets and time-lines, and facing challenges when it finally comes time to put your property on the market.

In the following sections, I'll introduce several important components to successful property flipping, elements that many first-time property flippers often struggle with or overlook entirely. But before we get into *how* to actually flip a property, you'll need to research and buy a physical property to flip. Chapter 5's discussion about residential property, commercial real estate, and raw land will be a helpful guide during this initial process, primarily because it introduces the most cost-effective, advantageous real estate pursuits currently available, and explains how you can take advantage of each opportunity. However, I'd highly recommend gearing all of your flipping endeavors toward residential property—this is the most popular, highly-demanded property type, and residential properties tend to move, generally speaking, much faster on the market than commercial real estate and raw land.

So, before you get started with the following steps and elements of flipping, know what property you'd like to flip, then purchase it. Once you've got that property under your belt, you're ready to tackle the following components to flipping.

Detailed budgets

By detailed budget, I mean knowing where and what your money is going toward, to the *last dollar*. Flipping becomes a very risky real estate pursuit when flippers stray from their budget—this is something that happens all too often. Not convinced? Watch any property flipping show on television. You'll see time and time again that flippers stray from budgets and struggle to complete renovations because they've used all of their funds. The worst thing you can do is take out *yet another loan* for your property. This shouldn't be a venture that puts you in debt for the next 10 years. It should require an investment, yes, but you should earn back your money, plus some, once you sell the property at the end of that 12-month period.

I'll admit, though, that creating a detailed budget, and sticking to it, can be both a trying task and a time-consuming one. A lot of thought and research will need to go into creating your budget. Plan to spend at least 15 hours of your time doing online research, browsing and speaking to employees at hardware/home improvement stores, and getting estimates from contractors. This is perhaps one of the most crucial components of flipping a property, so don't shy away from it, and don't be put off if you find yourself needing to put more than 15 hours into this research, budget-creating stage.

Here's another helpful tip to think about as you create your budget: it should be completed and agreed upon by all parties (you and anyone else who might be funding this property flip) *before* you start the actual flip. And when I say completed, I mean you should have a polished, neat, organized, and detailed piece of *real* paper in front of you that notes the details of each renovation, the cost (either the estimate you received or the amount you calculated during your research), and how much wiggle room, in dollar amount, that you have for each.

As you near completing this step, you should have some sort of idea about how much you intend to sell the property for. Keep in mind that you'll want to have all of the money that you put toward renovations returned to you at the end of this flip, plus some.

As you put all of this information together, however, be sure that your total budget is based on one year, but has some wiggle room in case your flip carries over a few extra (and perhaps unexpected) months. Remember, all of this should last just 12-months, ideally. Here are some vital costs that you'll want to calculate and understand while you construct this budget:

- Short-term loans needed to either purchase property or undergo renovations

- Property taxes

- Utilities (such as electricity, running water, plumbing, etc.)

- Cost of total materials and labor

- Intended sell price

Pre-established Schedules

Schedules, much like budgets, are very, *very*, important when it comes to successful property flipping. Without regimented schedules that aren't closely followed, a 12-month flip period all too often turns into a 2 or 3 year period of frustration, financial-stress, and emotional-drainage. Too many first-time, or even experienced, flippers run into these problems when they take their schedule for granted, or worse, choose to ignore it and go rouge. But going rouge is fatal to flipping property successfully. Creating and closely adhering to a regimented schedule is how you'll make it out of that 12-month flip period alive, well, and financially-sound.

Creating a schedule that details your flip project can be hard, though, especially when it's supposed to detail the events of your flip over the course of a 12-month period. To make this process of creating a schedule a little less daunting, I'd recommend:

1. Create 2 sets of 6 months schedules

2. Create 4 sets of 3 month schedules

3. Create 6 sets of 2 month schedules

4. Create 12 sets of 1 month schedules

5. Create a schedule for each week

It sounds like quite a bit of work, but starting broad at first, then narrowing down to a week-orientated schedule is your best bet. For example, your schedule for step #1 might look something like this:

January 2016-June 2016:

- Renovate living room, bedroom #1, bedroom #2

July 2016-Decemeber 2016:

- Renovate bedroom #3, kitchen, backyard

Your schedule for step #5, on the other hand, should be much more detailed and complex. It might look something like this:

January 2016, Week #1:

- Renovate living room

- o 1/1 – 1/3: 15x25 carpet replacement

- o 1/3 – 1/6: Knock down interior wall

- o 1/6 – 1/7: Add 10x 9 carpet to additional living room area

January 2016, Week #2:

- Renovate living room (continued)

  - o 1/8 – 1/12: New paint, all 4 interior walls

  - o 1/11 – 1/14: Replace windows, new paint on window frames

Notice how step #5 is *much more* specific than step #1. Specific dates are included, and certain renovation-related tasks are assigned to a specific date range. Essentially, what this schedule helps you do is this: set specific dates that each renovation will be done by so that you don't fall behind schedule. Keep in mind, though, that all of this scheduling should be started *and* completed before you begin the flip.

Set-backs are inevitable during this process, however, so it's vital that you establish a back-up plan, and therefore, create a back-up schedule. Or, if you can't afford to dedicate a few more hours of your time to creating another separate schedule, be sure to leave a few extra days of each month empty—task free. Having 2-3 days in each month that aren't fully scheduled means you can use these days to catch up on work that hasn't yet been completed, or give delayed projects the opportunity to catch up. In some cases, you'll find that certain projects can't be started until the project before it is finished. Take removing an interior wall as an example. If removing the wall is delayed, then your plans to add carpeting to that new, expanded area will be delayed, too, right? This is why small allotments of free time in your schedule are important to include.

You might also find it helpful to create a quick list of renovations that *must be completed* and renovations that *should be completed* within that 12-month period. This will help you set your priorities straight in case long delays occur or projects are put on hold. For example, you might find replacing the outdated kitchen cabinets more important than adding new baseboards to the kitchen, since the outdated kitchen cabinets are much more obvious and visually-displeasing. Replacing the kitchen cabinets will also contribute to your property's value more so than would new baseboards.

Buyer Interests

Once you've purchased a property, you should already have some sort of idea about who your intended consumer is. If you've purchases a 3-bedroom single-family home situated in a family-friendly suburban area, located within walking distance of the elementary school, then you can probably assume that your consumer will be a family with young, school-age children, looking for property in a quiet, friendly neighborhood. If you've purchased a high-end studio apartment located in the midst of the city's financial district, on the other hand, then you can probably assume that your buyer will be a professional couple or single individual who works in or near the city.

Once you make an educated guess about who your potential buyers might be (you should be thinking about this before or soon after you purchase your flip property), it's important that some, if not all, of your property renovations are done with them in mind. That is, if you know your buyers will probably be a young family, for example, then you'll want to gear your renovations in directions that cater to a family's interests. Improving the backyard by adding new grass, a fence, a small patio, and a deck might be something to consider if you think your buyers will be spending a lot of time outside with the family. Sticking with the family-buyer example, finishing the basement of the property might also be a wise investment to consider—families will appreciate walled, carpeted, and wire-free basements that give children additional play areas. Hopefully you see what I'm getting at here.

Sell It

Flipping a property can be done with the help of an agent, or entirely on your own. I mentioned this earlier in Chapter 2 when we discussed the pros and cons of working with an agent vs. working independently, but if it's your first-time flipping a property, I'd recommend pulling in the help of an agent, even if just part-time. Managing a flip in addition to learning how to *sell* your flipped property can be tricky, though not entirely impossible—the Realtor just makes it easier on *your* end.

If you are planning on flipping your property and putting it on the market on your own, you'll need to learn how to *sell* it—what to say and how to say it during open houses with potential buyers. An agent will know what to say already, though I'm afraid you'll have to learn. Fortunately, there are certain things that you *need* to know about and be able to explain when you discuss your property to potential buyers. Questions you'll need to be able to answer or speak in detail about include, but certainly aren't limited to:

- Year built
- Previous owners
- Neighborhood
- School systems

- Length of time on market

- Square feet

- Lot size

- Type of heating/cooling/etc. system in place

- Average cost of monthly utilities

- Key features (fireplaces, finished basements/attics, porch/deck, etc.

- If asking price is over/under market value

- Recent renovations

In addition to all of these elements, you'll also want to talk up your renovations. The whole point is to sell this property to your potential buyers, so *tell* them all that you've done during those past 12-months. Tell them what makes your property so great. Talk to them about what's been renovated, replaced, constructed, removed, and added.

You might also find it helpful to create organized, visually-appealing, and easy-to-read flyers or brochures about your property. These documents should include lists and pictures about what's been renovated, replaced, added, etc. It's important that your potential buyers learn about the property while they're currently there viewing it, but that they also have a reminder about the property's great features when they leave it, too.

Conclusion

At this point, you've hopefully learned a great deal about real estate—what exactly constitutes real estate, what your options are in the world of real estate, how to test your hand at property management, how to excel as an independent buyer and seller of real estate, what property types are the most advantageous to your personal cause, and how to successfully flip a property without the added frustrations and financial-drainage.

Although this book is by no means an extensive guide to real estate, it does provide a preview into what you can expect upon entering the world of appraisals, contingencies, negotiations, and commissions, or, in other words, real estate. Hopefully you've felt this way throughout your reading, too.

In Chapter 1, we began our conversation by introducing exactly what real estate was. We learned about real estate's pros and cons, alongside the terms appreciation and commission. In Chapter 2, I provided a brief overlook of your options in the world of real estate. We discussed your options of becoming an agent—and the step-by-step process of successfully doing so and securing your real estate license—and also explored the option of buying and selling real estate independently, or, without the assistance of a licensed agent.

In Chapter 3, I introduced a fairly new but rapidly growing alternative to real estate—AirBNB. However, you should have discovered that this doesn't always need to be an alternative to real estate. Posting and renting out your property to tourists and traveling professionals using AirBNB also serves as an excellent gateway into the world of real estate. You'll get a feel for how property management and interaction with clients works, and in the process, you'll hopefully gather a better understanding for what your involvement in the real estate world might be like. Next, chapter 4 was dedicated to those ambitious individuals who are interested in pursuing real estate endeavors independently. In this chapter, I introduced a helpful way to transition into this task, along with the pros and cons of this pursuit.

Following this, Chapter 5 discussed the three major forms of real estate—residential, commercial, and raw land—in more detail than we did earlier on in the book. In this section, I explained the definition of each property type, what to look for when you decide to pursue one or several property types, and how you'll generate the biggest profit during selling transactions. Chapter 6 concluded our conversation by discussing an up-and-coming topic in the real estate world—property flipping. In this section you learned about the 4 crucial elements of property flipping—creating detailed budgets, establishing schedules, catering to your potential buyer's interests, and learning to *sell* your property.

At this stage in the game, and after having read this book, your next task is to decide what option you want to pursue, and then pursue it. Although learning the ropes of real estate will certainly take some time, your best option is to dive in. Be eager to learn about the market, its movements, its patterns, and how it functions. Don't hesitate to seek guidance when you need it or ask for advice when it's wanted. I hope this book has helped you come to a more informed understanding of the basics of real estate, and that you pursue your endeavors with a greater sense of confidence and desire.

I wish you the best of luck in all your real estate and financial endeavors.

Made in the USA
Middletown, DE
03 April 2017